Ohm On The Range

Ohm On The Range

Robot and Computer Jokes

compiled by Charles Keller

illustrated by Art Cumings

Prentice-Hall , Inc.

Englewood Cliffs, New Jersey

For Nicole and Leigh

Text copyright © 1982 by Charles Keller
Illustrations copyright © 1982 by Art Cumings
All rights reserved. No part of this book
may be reproduced in any form, or by any means,
except for the inclusion of brief quotations in a review,
without permission in writing from the publisher.
Printed in the United States of America.
Prentice-Hall International, Inc., London
Prentice-Hall of Australia, Pty. Ltd., Sydney
Prentice-Hall Canada, Inc., Toronto
Prentice-Hall of India Private Ltd., New Delhi
Prentice-Hall of Japan, Inc., Tokyo
Prentice-Hall of Southeast Asia Pte. Ltd., Singapore
Whitehall Books Limited, Wellington, New Zealand

10 9 8 7 6 5 4 3

Library of Congress Cataloging in Publication Data
Keller, Charles. Ohm on the range.
Summary: A collection of robot and computer
jokes and riddles.
1. Riddles, Juvenile. 2. Computers—
Anecdotes, facetiae, satire, etc. 3. Automata—
Anecdotes, facetiae, satire, etc. [1. Riddles.
2. Computers—Wit and humor. 3. Robots—Wit
and humor] I. Cumings, Art, ill. II. Title.
PN6371.5.K39 1982   818.5402   82-7668
ISBN 0-13-633552-7   AACR2

What's a computer electrician's favorite song?
"Ohm on the Range."

What's the similarity between computers and robots?
Neither can play tennis.

What do you call a wristwatch worn in the twenty-first century?
A future-wrist-tick.

What did the robot say to the video space game?
"Hello, Beautiful."

I'm going to marry a robot girl.
Really? You're pretty ugly. How can she possibly see anything in you?
She's got X-ray eyes.

What has four legs but can't walk?
Two broken robots.

What do you get when you cross an elephant with a computer?
A five-ton know-it-all.

Did you hear about the robot who took the bus home?
No, what happened?
His owner made him take it back.

What do robots give their girl friends?
Assorted nuts.

Did you hear about the robot who couldn't get to sleep so he tried counting sheep?
Did that help?
No, his calculator made too much noise.

What do you call a robot with no ears?
I don't know, what?
Anything you want, because he can't hear you.

What do you call a computer that costs a lot of money but makes many mistakes?
A million error.

What do you call a computer with a brainstorm?
A washout.

What do you get when you cross a blender with a calculator?
A mixed solution.

Why did the teenage robot bring home steel wool?
So his mother could knit him a car.

What do you call a computer that splits grams?
A gram cracker.

What happened to the robot who stared at the watch too long?
He got clock-eyed.

What did one calculator say to the other calculator?
"You can count on me."

They're looking for responsible people to work on computers in the space program.
Then I'm the right person for that job. In the last place I worked, any time something went wrong with a computer, I was responsible.

What did the computer say when the spaceship landed on Mars instead of Venus?
"I didn't planet that way."

What goes clomp, swish-clomp, swish-clomp, swish?
A robot with a wet tennis sneaker.

What did the robot say to the magnet.
"I find you very attractive."

Why did the robot play with the flying saucer?
He thought it was a Frisbee.

What would you give to a 1,000 pound robot?
Anything he wants.

Who invented the first mechanical man?
Frank N. Stein.

What do you call a large computer that hitchhikes?
A two-and-a-half-ton pickup.

Did you hear about the computer that went "tick, tick, tick"?
No.
It was the tock of the town.

How can you tell if a robot is visiting your house?
Look to see if his motorcycle is parked outside.

What kind of car does a computer drive?
A Volts Wagon.

What time is it when a robot sits on your car?
Time to buy a new car.

One of our robots was hit by a meteor.
Was he hurt?
No, but he was really spaced out.

What do you get when you cross a robot with a Boy Scout?
A robot who helps old people across the street.

I would like to become a space computer engineer.
Do you think you can pass the test?
Sure, I took up space in school.

If it takes two computers two hours to do a problem, how long would it take five computers to do it?
Why should they do it at all? The two computers just did it.

Where does a robot go when he loses a hand?
To a secondhand shop.

I have a rare old video game that once belonged to Benjamin Franklin.
But there were no video games in Franklin's time.
That's what makes it so rare.

Did you hear about the stick-up on the giant computer?
No, what happened?
Some kid threw it up there.

What do you get when you cross a robot with a mouse?
Huge holes in your wall.

What did one computer electrician say to the other?
"Let's get together and discuss current events."

Did you hear about the insects that computer analysis found in the moon material at NASA?
No, what were they?
Lunarticks.

The computer broke down because of a short circuit.
Well, why didn't they lengthen it?

I wish I had enough money to buy a giant computer.
Why do you want a giant computer?
I don't. I just want the money.

Why did the robot on the spaceship lose his job?
He got fired.

Did you hear about the computer that is almost human?
No, how does it work?
When it makes a mistake, it blames it on someone else.

What did the robot say to the coffee machine?
"Honey, you sure make a good cup of coffee."

Why didn't it do the scientist any good to put an
ad in the paper when he lost his robot?
Why?
His robot never reads the papers.

Did you hear about the computer that swallowed a
yo-yo?
It gave the same answer ten times.

What do you get when you cross a goat with a
robot?
An animal that eats a path to your door.

What does a mechanical frog say?
"Robot, robot."

Because our modern spaceships are run by computers, they can do anything a bird can do and more.
I'd like to see one sleeping on a telephone wire with his head tucked under his wing.

What did one computer punch card say to the other?
"I'm holier than thou."

What's the easiest way to count cows?
On a cowculator.

Do you know what robots have on their saddles
when they go out riding at night?
No, what?
Communication saddle lights.

What did the electrician say when his computer
was late?
"Wire you insulate?"

Did you hear that they invented an electric vampire?
No, how does it work?
It runs on bat-teries.

Why did the robot salute the refrigerator?
Because it was General Electric.

What did the computer say to the electricity?
"I get a charge out of you."

Our computer did the same problem five times.
Good, what did you get?
Here are the five answers.

What do you get when you cross a lobster with a calculator?
A snappy answer.

Did you hear about the robot who stayed up all night to see where the sun went when it went down?
No, what happened?
If finally dawned on him.

What do you call a robot that can do card tricks on a bicycle?
A wheeler dealer.

What would happen if a ten-foot robot sat in front of you at the movies?
You'd miss the picture.

Why did the scientist put itching powder on his computer when he had a problem?
So he could start from scratch.

What goes, "Ha, ha, ha, plop"?
A robot laughing his head off.

What do you get when you cross a large robot with a fly?
I don't know.
I don't know either. But if it lands on you, you're a goner.

What do robots take for a cough?
Robot-tussin.

What do they do with old bowling balls?
They give them to robots to shoot marbles with.

What has two heads, three arms, and three legs?
A robot with spare parts.

Why did the robot eat electric light bulbs at noontime?
Because he wanted a light lunch.

This new computer will do half the work of your company.
Good, I'll take two of them.

Why should you never say 288 to a computer?
Because it is two gross.

What's the difference between a robot and a mailbox?
I don't know, what?
I'd hate to send you to mail a letter.

What do you get when you cross a robot with a kangaroo?
Great big holes all over Australia.

What did the computer say when it ran out of electricity?
"AC come, AC go."

Can your robot telephone from a spaceship?
Of course. Who can't tell a phone from a spaceship.

What do you get when you cross a midget with a computer?
A short circuit.

What did the digital clock say to its mother?
"Look, Ma, no hands."

What did the robot say to the piano keyboard?
"Wipe that silly grin off your face."

Do you know where I can get a bowling ball and a milk can?
No, why?
I'm trying to make a roll-on deodorant for robots.

What goes "snap, crackle, pop"?
A computer with a short circuit.

According to our computer, that planet on the right of the spaceship is Mars.
Then I suppose the other one is Pa's?

How do you make a robot light?
Plug his finger in a socket.

How do you catch a unique robot?
I don't know, how?
Unique up on him. How do you catch a tame robot?
I don't know the answer to that either.
The tame way.

What did the robot say when the sports car ran into him?
"How many times have I told you kids not to play in the street?"

What did the robot say when he found a young prince in his soup?
"Waiter, there's a heir in my soup."

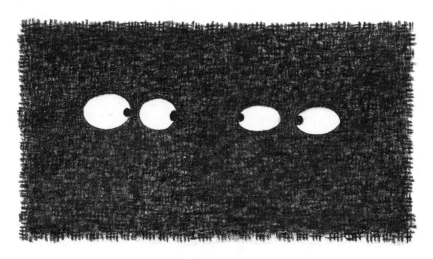

**Hello, Control, our computer just landed us on the
dark side of the moon, and we have a problem.**
What's the problem, Spaceship?
We forgot to bring the flashlights.

Why did the robot wear sunglasses?
Because with all these robot jokes around, he didn't
want to be recognized.

What did they write on the robot's tombstone?
"Rust in Peace."